# The 4000 Nights of New York in 1988

# &

# Mouth Music

Peter Urpeth

The 4000 Nights of New York in 1988

& Mouth Music

# Contents

# Notes and Acknowledgements

I would like to thank all those who have supported my writing and given me encouragement and advice over the years.

I dedicate this book to my family and friends, especially to my wife, Chrissie Bel, who has provided me with so much support over all of these years.

I would like to thank photographer Stephen Salmieri for permission to use his beautiful photo 'SoHo 1988' as the cover image for this book. Check out his work at - *salmieriphotographs.com*

My thanks to Kat Francois for her expert guidance in the development of this work - *www.katfrancois.com*

Some of the poems in this collection have previously appeared in poetry magazines, journals and anthologies.

The poems in Mouth Music and the earlier poems were published as an ebook in 2015 under the title Overlapping. These have been extensively revised and edited for this collection.

The 4000 Nights of New York in 1988 was first performed at Dark Skies Festival, An Lanntair, Stornoway, Isle of Lewis, in February 2022.

The Vision & On This Autumn Day were first published in Northwords, 1997. The Vision was published under the title Da Shelladh.

Winter Blood & Scald - a Mouth Rune - was first published in issue 18 of Northwords, 1998.

Red Kites at Docherty - was first published in the anthology Riptide, Two Ravens Press, 2007.

Mouth Music, The Plover & The Emptying, The Finding were first published in Northwords Now, Issue 13, Autumn 2009.

Overlapping was first published in Northwords Now, Issue 13 Autumn 2009.

Close Worlds - was first published by Island Life Magazine, Stornoway Gazette, in 2009

Erosion & The Dunlin were first published in Cencrastus No 58, Autumn 1997.

All other poems are published here for the first time.

The phrase 'brother to brother, and brother to brother' in Quixote in Dalston is a brief quote from, and homage to, Marlon Riggs and his 1989 documentary, 'Tongues Untied' (*Frameline / California Newsreel*)

The narrative of the troubadour at First and First in the poem The 4000 Nights of New York in 1988, grew from a improvisation on some lines by Oliver Lake on his album 'The Matador of 1st & 1st' (Passin' Thru, 1995).

8

# The 4000 Nights
# of New York
# in 1988

# Quixote in Dalston


Quixote came to Dalston
in a leopard's hide
and slow-muled the lane,
taut and tilting the E8 ride,
and tongued the grove
out of way-out jazz
in the Duke's dive -
that scene of dykes and bois
and art jazz noise,
Dudu was in the back room
riffing Township licks,
behind every back beat
swings Moholo kicks,
every solo was a rage of
lips and fingers,
the breath of saints
and the breath of sinners
breath to breath
and breath to breath,
and brother to brother
brother to brother,
and blue notes
for Dyani's ghost,
deep sonorous
bass tones of longing,
all red bowed and lover's lips
singing in the shadows on
the Balls Pond Road...

and sure we're knocking rums
for every angel sunk,
Quixote was a Valentino punk
and perfect bound
in her inked skin,
a peroxide diamond
in a ring of tin…
and sure we're down
with the small talk graces,
one line sonnets,
lipstick traces on rose
red chasers with
intimate intimations,
whispering sweet
pirate songs
heard on a whistle,
hauled from the guts
of a detuned fiddle,
heard on an Orphic lyre
drowned by the furies
in a Mare Street bar,
and the barmaid's
a mermaid from down
London Fields,
all combs and mirrors
and Neptune's shield,
weeping salt shanties,
and we're all lost souls
with a crushed ice fate,
dying in the shoulder-clinking
coolness of the moment -

life's a wake,
life's your wake
pull up a stool.

In this Hackney constellation
each star's a stanza bright,
a glimmered hope
on a dark night,
a twinkle twinkle
for the dreamers
wandering under avenues
of London plains.

There is a poetry
in sharps and blades
and inking points
and water shades,
there is a poetry
in the forge marks
at the meeting edge
of our difference,
and we laid serene
as carp in those pictures
of the floating world
you'd stretch across
your back,
in the eye pools
of pink koi drifting
beneath an arch
of white chrysanthemums,
beneath the cherry blossoms
dying after the last bloom

of spring, listening
to fingers moving lightly
over skin, the sound of reeds
shaking in the winter wind,
the sound of bamboo swaying
in a forest of bamboo.

# Altered Sensualities I

When Lethe
with peroxide flowed
and our hands
did hold cupped
a thirst for nothing
but this shroud
of words and music,
a serenade
for our blank descent,
and you sent out
into London's grey facade
lines like glowing ashes
with no memory
for their flames,
and the cold light
of a winter's day
that came.

These words,
each sensual
when intoned
in oratories
of scored ink
bemoaned the limit
of us to us,
then silence
once again.

## Altered Sensualities II

Reading in a London room -

the autumn light

is not perfect

for the page,

as it fades lines absorb

time and time

for a moment then

evening sparks

bright animations of stillness

across your face,

your wide eyes moving

like twin bright moons spooning

across a dark and infinite sky.

# Every Inch of Skin

Every inch of skin
you gave,
you gave
to the work
of change,
change because
you were scared
of everything,
change because
you could bleed
no more desire's blood
you broke out
its clotted vein,
broke it with
the neat incision
of intent,
pulled out its vine
tore the spine
that binds us
so tightly
in ourselves.

You said that you did not
own your body -
you were always their's
for the taking,
and take they did,

but you pushed
beyond to survive
in an economy
of excess,
you formed a manifesto
of the I, and made
a promise to give
too much.

Everything the eye can see
is given, everything that skin
can feel is given,
but not by love
or curiosity
for the prowess
of the senses,
but by form and law
and warnings
of a bloody fate,
they push within us
a vocabulary of hate
that is not anywhere
on autocorrect.

This work of change
is never done with,
this work of change
is never over.

You were not,
or never will be,
forgiven,

you made the line
the word
the single syllable
of the I, one
vertical stroke pointing
to the universe
within, a slim, mile-high
gesture of defiance,
elegant and poised,
a multitude of presences
both wall and gate
and sign, divine
totem of the self.

The poetry of ligatures
you practised,
free mannered figures,
phrase dances
of the breath
that open to the beats
that swing,
meditations
on a revolution
in desire from within,
change, because
you were scared
of everything.

# The 4000 Nights of New York in 1988

Few could see hope
in the dark burn
of night,
its cold flames
do not conjure pictures
of comfort for the innocent
but interrogate and trap the soul
in stories of destruction,
narratives born and risen
from smoke,
in the identities we imagined
for ourselves
to make our love possible

You spoke of love once
as though it were
a steady lantern flame
protected in its fragile
transparency from the eyes
of onlookers,
and you spoke of the comfort
you found watching
the distant glimmer
of plane lights
passing high
across a dark sky
as you drifted to sleep,

and the comforting indifference
of the passing car lights
on far Williamsburg
or Washington

We knew the lip flames
of strangers
taken not caring
for the chained
rosary tomes of doubt
or the flamed beads
of tomorrow
hand-turned in night time's
blue reflections -

and we walked
the skin bridge of Brooklyn
in search of tattoos
in memory of us,
we saw tourists
taking photographs
of a dead hobo
in the avenue gutter,
we saw Mnemosyne
in the Bowery
who, with a poker, tends
an oil can broiler
coaxing tindered logs
to free bright cinders
into that rare air
which glowed
for but a moment

then grew old,
and old they died,
ancient in a moment
of the day that too was dying

Flame consumes us -
flame consumes us
in veils of love,
flame consumes us
in veils of endless whys
and whys and whys,
flame consumes us
in veils of love -
at First and First a troubadour
sings ballads to the beat box
of car wipers for a dime
and there's a dancer north
who writhes to the clatter grate
of sounds from the overhead
rattle rail of the A line,
and all the world fits
in that beatbox -
the A line's a beatbox
the sidewalk is a beatbox
the park and seventh avenue
are a beatbox,
the Bronx and Harlem
Brooklyn and Queens,
the Bronx and Harlem
Brooklyn and Queens
the Hudson and the Village,
the Staten Island Ferry

is a beatbox drifting
by liberty's flame,
reflected in this blue
dissolve of memory

So this is for us, to us
in memoriam of flame
and the 4000 nights
of New York in 1988.

# Morton Street

The ash leaves
are yellowing
on Morton Street
just now,
and the walk-ups
to the brownstone homes,
in unison with the fall,
pull back a yard it seems
to let the canopy
of light turn grey,
to let summer's glory
fade away in grace.

There is quiet here
but for the Hudson's lap,
quiet but for the writer's
type tapped on
feint-lined pages,
the ribboned clicks and claps
that crept from the gaps
in first storey windows,
the roll and rasp,
the grip and curse of
the misjudged return,
sonnets for the city
that always weeps…

Seventh Avenue is a chorus
of car horns and complaint -
who cares buddy if the bus
won't start
or the trash cart rolls
so slowly to the grate
that you'll be late
for nothing or nobody
that matters?
who cares if we can pass
in a moment of the eye
in the time it takes
for ink to dry?
and that you cannot cry
you say because
this was never nothing
anyway, and so what
you bought a ticket
to goodbye,
you didn't bank
on us at all…

This New York journal
is a book of thieves,
not garnished with
last summer's leaves
but block redactions
penned and scrawled,
involuntary memories
too bitter for this pen
to hold,
its white lined spine

is levered by old tickets
jammed on days and dates
we don't recall -
a stub to The Poet's Marathon
at St Mark's Hall,
Ginsberg reading Howl
to Larry Fagin,
Philip Glass playing minimalism
to a Californian pagan,
wrist bands to see art punks
in Lower East side dives
and bills for cocktails
that speak easy of demise,
negatives of some photos taken
in a park-side hotel
basement.

What do these days
or minutes or hours
matter in this earthly roll?
Lines should be like razors
fresh with blood
but not your own,
it is the passing scent
and the poetry of lament
that memories hold
not chronologies
of the bold
or stepping stones
or crucial dates
but destinies of fate
sensed and grasped

in seconds…
we never were,
we never could be
anything but over…

We revisit
what we know
on unseen repeat
like the leaves
that each year
grow and fall
on Morton Street.

# East River Blues

*from a New York journal...*

Walking...walking...walking

from Vanderbilt YMCA
on 47th street between 2nd and 3rd
I turn right and right
to go down town,
the heat is stifling,
the thick, still air
from FDR Avenue
is unbreathable,
suffocations with every step...

*On this summer's day*
*all I hear and all I see*
*is the east river blues,*
*the east river blues,*
*the blue that flows,*
*the blue above,*
*the blue within,*
*the ghosts of loss*
*and struggle*
*everywhere*
*in this city's*
*blue shadows*

On Second Avenue,
a light-yellowed
hand-written postcard
is taped to the inside
of the front window
of a Ma and Pa store,
a downtown punk and his crew
have made their move,
in blue-inked scrawl it reads:

*We're looking for a drummer -*
*must be dedicated, hard-hitting,*
*in it for life,*
*willing to die naked in an alley*
*for your anti-art,*
*outcasts and social rejects*
*preferred but not essential.*

Walking west I pass
the chained entrance
of the bookstore where
in 1965 Milford Graves
played Saturdays
on the mezzanine floor,
Yara of the mind and
Yoruba is the score,
spontaneous improvisations
of words, not book-like,
no spine-grip boundaries
of form, no commodity
of knowledge
it's here and now, these words,

these songs,
this union of purpose,
these songs of skin,
this knowing that skin
can sing, that skin
has its own memory
of this minute, this hour, this day
this year, of a thousand years past,
a memory of five hundred years,
each tick or tock,
each click or beat
each chime separated
by an ocean of silence
and time, from beginning to end
a memory that breaks open
shackles,
a memory that cannot mend
the harm, but which is formative
of the necessary conditions
of change...

*On this summer's day*
*all I hear and all I see*
*is the east river blues,*
*the east river blues,*
*the blue that flows,*
*the blue above,*
*the blue within,*
*the ghosts of loss*
*and struggle*
*everywhere in this city's*
*blue shadows*

At the gateway
to Peter Stuyvesant Village,
I think of Lee Lorch,
Professor of maths,
the grandchild of
German Jewish immigrants
who fled the Rhine
for the Hudson.
I think of Lee Lorch
who organised the first
racially-integrated union
of public school teachers
in Louisville.
I think of Lee Lorch
who was sacked
from his academic post
at City College
for his fight to end
the institutional policy
of racial exclusion
of black US army veterans
from his home estate
which was built
with charitable status
as a home for returning
WW2 serviceman,
so long as they were white.
I think of Lee Lorch
who got a new job
at Penn State University
but did not give up
his flat in Stuyvesant village

but lent it instead
to a black veteran soldier
and his family
to be his guests,
and so circumvented
the village's discriminatory policies,
his actions came to the attention
of his employer,
who did not renew his tenure
and who said that Lorch's actions were:

*"extreme, illegal, and immoral,*
*and damaging to the public relations*
*of the college."*

I think of Lee Lorch
who faced down and refused
to cooperate with
the House Anti-American
Activities Committee,
who accused him of being
a communist.
I think of Lee Lorch
who did not defend
his case on the 5th amendment
right to silence,
but on the 1st amendment
right to the freedom of speech,
and who was then sacked
from his job at Fisk University
for his unrelenting views
as a socialist.

*On this summer's day,*
*all I hear and all I see*
*is the east river blues,*
*the east river blues,*
*the blue that flows,*
*the blue above,*
*the blue within*
*the ghosts of loss*
*and struggle*
*everywhere*
*in this city's*
*blue shadows.*

I think of Lee Lorch
and his wife Grace
living in Little Rock, Arkansas,
who was sacked
for his attempt
to enrol their daughter
in a black segregated school
following the outlawing
of racial discrimination
in the education system
of the land.
I think of Grace Lorch
who protected Elizabeth Eckford,
a 15 year old girl of colour,
from a violent
and braying mob
of white supremacists,
who tried to stop her
and eight other children

from entering the town's
whites-only school
to enrol for their studies -
Arkansas State guards
would block their road,
Arkansas State guards
in full battle dress
would block that road
fearful of the power
of a 15-year-old girl.
I think of Elizabeth Eckford
and her friends, who,
under the protection
of Eisenhower's national guard
would return to those gates
and would take their
rightful places
in those classrooms.
I think of all nine children
who, within a year
had fled that school,
those supposed halls
of education,
the victims of a relentless
campaign of hate,
a campaign heard
in every corridor,
heard in every gym hall,
heard at lunchtimes
and at play,
heard at sports
and in assemblies,

heard in the silence
of birthday party invites
not sent,
heard in the campaign
to drive them out,
heard in the campaign
that drove them out,
they drove them out
for being black and
for wanting to learn
like any other kids.
I think of Elizabeth Eckford
who would never recover
from the experiences
she endured in those days.
I think of Grace Lorch,
who, too, was called before
the House Anti-American
Activities Committee
for her actions.
I think of Lee and Grace Lorch
who'd find
unexploded dynamite
concealed in the garage
of their Little Rock home
as white supremacists tried
to punish them
for their activism.
I think of the 21
black American women
who, prior to 1980,
had achieved doctorates

in maths, and Lorch
had taught three of them
and encouraged countless more
to pursue their love
of math and science.

*On this summer's day,*
*all I hear and all I see*
*is the east river blues,*
*the east river blues,*
*the blue that flows,*
*the blue above,*
*the blue within*
*the ghosts of loss*
*and struggle*
*everywhere*
*in this city's*
*blue shadows.*

I turn from the grand
arched gates of that village,
and run and run down
Avenue A,
a placard at the gate
of St Brigid's Church,
states:

*"Gentrification is class war -*
*No Peace without Housing"*

...and in the hot August glare
know that the shards

37

of Tompkins Square Park
will burn once more,
will burn as the city police,
their badges concealed,
will ride on horse back
in a night of rage
to baton charge and beat
the homeless,
they'll beat the crowds
who will gather to fight
for their lives,
to fight fire
with fire,
but the force
they will face
will be too much,
the force will be
too much,
the force
will clear the park,
the police will beat you
until you know
you cannot die there
alone, claimed by your
drug use, you cannot
freeze to death there
in your makeshift tent
surrounded by the only people
who care for you,
you cannot die there,
you have no right
to die there, cold

in defiance of architect's
blue prints for
gentrified developments
on that land,
these news homes
will not become
for you, a first or second
home for your
all-American dream,
you cannot die there
forgotten or forsaken
by your family,
you have no right
to die there in pain,
this is not your
neighbourhood,
this is not your home,
there is no pathway here
for you, no access here
for you to the land
of the free.
I think of Tompkins Square Park
back in 1873,
where once before
starving and penniless
workers were baton-charged
by mounted police
as they strove to secure
a fair deal on pay
and a chance to live
and work without fear
of destitution...

*On this summer's day,*
*all I hear and all I see*
*is the east river blues,*
*the east river blues,*
*the blue that flows,*
*the blue above,*
*the blue within*
*the ghosts of loss*
*and struggle*
*everywhere*
*in this city's*
*blue shadows.*

# Lullaby for the Self in Crisis

Hush, be still
all troubles pass
hold on hold on
hold on hold on
my heart,
as long as you can
the moon and stars
don't fall
at once,
so rock and sway
and sleep will come,
so rock and sway
and sleep will come,
the day with tender light
will break,
then rise and rise
and rise my heart
for living's sake,
hold on hold on
hold on hold on
my heart,
the moon and stars
don't fall at once.

# Pavane (For a Dead Writer)

*For KA*

I'm snared in the wire
of your kennings,
trapped at the boundaries
we scented around
our buried bed,
in that place of soft down
where we hid amongst
the moss and roots
of wine and needles
in those few November days.

I remember the comfort
of the fibre we ripped
from our tears,
and the coarseness
of the twine
still in the seams,
knotted but frayed
beyond the knot,
beyond retying.

The drug novenas,
the neck nape,
the voice nape,
the mirrored face,
the mirrored voice,
the plainchant smile,

and all the while
you rode Quixote
that journey of lines
and night fires,
calling on the burnt
and the scarred,
those you loved
and could not leave
behind.

Manhattan,
at sunset in the Village
the Hudson houses glow gold,
the Hudson glows gold,
the white bling of far Liberty
is cold and hanging,
if you look closely
you can see
the high rail she holds
with tired fingers,
then slowly each unfurls
until nothing holds that rail
and we are fallen,
and we said never
to talk of it,
because death is
but a moment of the tongue,
and lips are always silent
anyway, just shapes of words
like pastry cutters
fixed in stars and os.

In Manhattan,
you glowed gold,
with blond roots,
with black roots,
at dusk, like a bat unfurling,
you quivered for the cold
till you flew out
into that gold air,
high above the village
and the east side,
high above the strip bar
you worked
for dollars at a time,
high above the theatre
where you read
your words,
high into the dark sky
of longing.

There is chaos in Liberty,
there is chaos in the silence of lips,
there is chaos in the death of tongues,
there is chaos in the moment,
there is chaos in roots,
there is chaos in the voice nape,
there is chaos in night fires,
there is chaos in the mirror face.

The drug novenas,
the neck nape,
the voice nape,
the mirrored face,

the mirrored voice,
the plainchant smile,
and all the while you ride
that journey of night fires,
calling on the burnt
and the scarred,
those you loved
and had to leave behind.

The drug novenas,
the neck nape,
the voice nape,
the mirrored face,
the mirrored voice,
the plainchant smile,
and all the while you ride
that journey of night fires,
calling on the burnt
and the scarred,
those you loved
and had to leave behind.

# Mouth Music

# Winter Blood

The bloods of winter
warm in the river's flow,
as dusk's cold, low moon
dissolves its clot of light
in that folding glow,
where tree sap
spilt in a storm,
drifts in corms
over rock silts
flowing in the
river's crura.

My fingers claw
at that river bed
searching for what
is buried there,
and I am prone then
as the river breaks
about me,
and I am
its new island.

Winter brings its timbers
down upon me -
in light that is but vapour
then is gone
in ice that binds and cracks

the plover's song -
and I shed this body,
this island land,
and lie on dry ground,
vulnerable
to the hooded crows,
until new flesh
grows about me.

# The Vision

The bodies of the drowned
lay where the bird-tide
had left its kerf, and
where storm-wrenched
seaweed was scattered
in tresses, a colony
of gash-finned seals
that died with slate-eyed pity
amongst shallow pools
the ebb forgot.

They lay beneath
a sigh of cloud,
beak-carved,
mute to the roup of skuas,
their hands reddened
with rock blood.

I took a fist full of the sand
from where they lay,
and held it until
it was again a boulder
of wind-cut granite
falling to the sea,
then another fist of sand
I held until it was a stone
journeying in a river

far inland,
and I held the river
until it rose
as a mountain glacier
burdened with a moraine
as it clove the glens.

Beneath a sigh of cloud,
my hands reddened
with rock blood,
I laid the bodies
of the drowned
in a field of stones.

# On This Autumn Day

The river flows
where the mountain puts it,
amongst gaunt rocks
that knarr the gorge,
and where the air heaves
loam scalds from
the forest floor.

On this autumn day,
the river flows iron-thick
as leg blood,
a flat silt force
through lowland plains.

In the high corrie,
where bare ferns wake
cogged in morning ice,
and where white heather smoulders
a forgotten red,
I mark the ground
and light the sky with fire
to greet this autumn dawn,
where the river
is at peace with
the mountain.

# Plover

Plover
wandering
like a banished monk
on the moor,
show me what you see
from your tummock,
tell me what you hear
at night in the darkness
so that I can learn
from the bog.

I envy you, plover,
running bare-foot
beyond the road end,
and your low, sure flight
by the river bend,
and do you know
your belly's black?
And why do you not
answer me plover
when I call to you?
Why do you ask me
why I live in a house
when the land is open
and the sky is as free
as burn water?

Why do you ask me
why I will not be
your neighbour?

I cannot whistle away the snow, Plover,
I am not the clay bird of god, Plover,
I am not free like you, Plover,
I am not free.

# Mouth Music

If the net breaks
we'll fish from the shore,
If the pipe reed splits
we'll sing instead,
If the singer is mute
we'll feed her seeds,
If the drum skin slackens
we'll stamp our feet.

If the peat is wet
we'll burn the creel,
If the berries shrivel
we'll eat the stems,
If the axe is blunt
we'll burn the books,
If the oar blade breaks
we'll hope for wind.

If the salmon dies
we'll never know,
If the heather burns
we'll sleep on bracken,
If the plover keens
we'll weep at night.
If we talk with the crows
we'll know our fate.

If the high tide turns
we'll gather kelp,
If the loon wails
we'll beat a path,
If we send word
the distance is shorter,
If we walk at night
we'll arrive by dawn.

If the crop fails
we'll gather at the shore,
If the nest is empty
we'll chew on feathers,
If the neck bone breaks
we'll set it by sunlight,
If the fruit is bitter
we'll blame the root.

If we bury what we have
we'll neither waste nor thrive,
If we shout down the well
there'll be weed in the burn,
If we sing on the machair
there'll be haar at the coast,
If we break the silence
we'll keep our tongues.

# Scald - A Mouth Rune

*For Kristjana Gunnars*

To you
who cut the Winter Rune
deep into the bark
of the tallest birch.

To you
who soaked a bird corpse
in pine sap
to make a winter lamp.

To you
who lived
by the silent histories
of the work of hands.

To you,
who read the blood words
written in the marrow-archive.

To you,
I give this word drum,
To you,
I give this owl bone beater,
To you,
I give this mouth rune.

# Bard of Hidden Things

*In memory of Torcuil MacRath, Bard of Grimshader*

I'll remember you standing
by the old gate in the new wall,
your hands raking caorans for the fire,
your eyes seeing far out
over Loch Urnabhaigh,
moving not on known ground
but watching for that territory
of close worlds you knew
in squints and glances,
for you had the quick sight
of the knowing.

I'll remember when you said,
'there's something wrong
when two lochs have the same name',
and how you stacked the Earth's words
at your door for the winter fire
burning in your memory
of a thousand years.

I'll remember you,
Bard of Hidden Things,
who knew that all true bards
must walk two paths at once,
learning the dialects of silence
in the tongues of the buried,
in which nothing ends.

# The Emptying, The Finding

*for Norrie Bissell*

You soussed your tongue
in the Clyde,
rode corporation buses
like a curragh
to tenement closes,
sowed dulse in rusted pans
for winter milking,
then set sail
for the light out west,
knowing well the old charts
of the Dumbarton Road.

On Luing,
the Bàird Cladaich
brag and chatter,
their gonys bobbing
keel-less over the sands,
and the terns
- Sternus Paradisaea -
(one summer flying,
two summers feeding),
worry over the verses
of a iorram they learned
in the waves of long back,
when there was just one word
for poetry and song.

On Luing,
the poet finds silence
in local abundance
bunched like Sea Pinks
on that mile of shore,
as hardy of the salt wind
as his own words,
fine for the emptying
and the finding.

# Peewit, My Son

I see him in a dream,
he's walking slowly
from me,
not checking
if I'm close behind,
he's done with all of that.

Noon, and he's out
stalking by the old fence,
moving so as not to disturb
the call and fall
of the peewit rolling
above the croft.

He stands,
held in that moment of time,
dazzled by the flight
of the bird, and I see
he's more child
than ever.

# Red Kites At Docherty

Above the fallen folly,
amongst the ballet holds
of the Scots Pine stands,
kite is silence gliding,
a russet hue skimmed
on the flat blue
of this winter day

We counted them,
three or five,
talon-grappling
in a stall of wings,
full of the fury-tangle
of the prodigal.

Once exiled
from these
haunted spaces,
they left these skies
burnished with vastness
until a fancy ancestor
returned, with half a memory
for the place.

# Overlapping

At St Aulas
in keeping
with the oral traditions
of wave birds,
the cormorants
speak Holy Norse
and the guillemots
have the Gaidhlig,
the gannets know Norn
and the black backs
staunch Doric,
the red legs have mostly Welsh
the kittiwakes some Cant
there's a crake in the dunes
who calls Xhosa,
and a goose
fluent in Inupiaq,
and the little auk,
who once took a vow
of silence
has weakened
for its love of words,
and the overlapping
of tongues by the shore.

# Hamon

*A sequence on the blade markings of the Kitana*

## Sugu

Even in wrought ores,
there is a poetry

## Sanbonsugi

In Torridon
of the grey ashes
I thought of the
tempered edge
of our joining,
and saw three cedars
in a cloud of days

## Tōran

The thousand gates
of enlightenment,

The thousand knots
in knowing,

The billowing
of a thousand reeds
at Dalmore.

# Earlier Poems

# Erosion

A sodden stook of ewe
gnawed at the spade-split
turnips laying in the field,
an acre of fodder roots,
plough-gashed
and mud smeared
as unearthed skulls,
forever biting the tongue.

Rain-blotted mosses
furred the few turned
boulders,
but there was none,
and never had been,
on the spikes of scree
that edged the wall.

In a copse of conifers
on the far flank,
where the land sunk
in a slump
of saturated ground,
I heard the wind blow
or was it the fierce noise
of erosion I heard
upon those stones?

that obstinate will of nature
and one true bond
of time and matter,
is tangible here,
in this soak
of February light,
on this landscape,
growing it all
in silence,
from the marrow
of an outcrop.

# Dunlin

The weather had been fierce
that March, bringing a late
shake of snow to the slopes
of Driesh.

When the snow had done
falling, the wind stayed on
clamping the lungs
of the horses that stood
motionless in those
sodden fields.

Panting, the dog
ran on before us
as we walked, then,
frantic and with
a sudden lurch,
he ferreted eagerly
in the heather
as we dropped
below the ridge
of the hill,
and returned to heel.

He dropped a dunlin
at our feet, halting us
on the path,
and waited

above his carrion
eager for some praise.

The dunlin lay there
dead, I guessed,
a day or two,
its body still a soft, limp
dislocation,
its one visible eye
hard and black
and flaking where
it had dried
in the early frost.

# About the Author

Peter Urpeth was born in London in 1963. He is a writer and musician now living in the Outer Hebrides of Scotland.

His poetry has been published in numerous poetry magazines and journals, including Cencrastus and Northwords Now.

His novel, Far Inland, was published by Polygon, Edinburgh in 2006.

*peterurpeth.com*

Printed in Great Britain
by Amazon